Generis
PUBLISHING

Employment Equity Act in South Africa: An Analytical Review from 1998 – 2022

Ivan Steenkamp

Title: Employment Equity Act in South Africa: An Analytical Review from 1998 – 2022

ISBN: 979-8-89248-142-7

Author: Ivan Steenkamp

Cover image: https://pixabay.com/

Publisher: Generis Publishing
Online orders: www.generis-publishing.com
Contact email: info@generis-publishing.com

Table of Contents

List of Tables

List of Figures

Abstract

South Africa is still considered the most economically, ethnically, and culturally diverse country in the world. Ensuring that workers enjoy a level of fairness and equality in the workplace the Employment Equity Act (EEA) No. 55 of 1998 was passed into law. The purpose of the Act is to protect the rights of workers against any form of discrimination by their employers.

This law also aims to correct past injustices by implementing affirmative action measures.

The Minister of Employment of Labour in South Africa recently amended the EEA of 1998 in order to regulate both sector-specific Employment Equity (EE) targets and the compliance criteria for the issuing of EE Compliance Certificates in terms of Section 53 of the EEA. These amendments will come into effect on September 1, 2023, and aim to increase opportunities for historically disadvantaged individuals, such as marginalised racial and gender groups, by increasing their workplace representation. Consequently, employees from these groups may have greater employment and career advancement opportunities. This study examines the impact and gaps of the EEA from its inception in 1998 to 2022, as well as the number of EEA reports submitted by designated employers to the South African Department of Employment and Labour in accordance with schedule 4 of the Act. For the purposes of affirmative action provisions, only employers with 50 or more employees will be deemed designated employers as of 1 September 2023. Total annual revenue will no longer be a factor. The focus between 2019 and 2022 will be briefly on determining the impact of the COVID-19 pandemic on the South African labour force, employed by the designated companies, that need to report on EE targets.

This research project used a mixed-method research approach. This approach combined qualitative and quantitative research methods to collect and evaluate the data for this study. This study is based on the analysis of a series of documents and secondary data obtained from various sources for the period 1998-2022.

The research questions are (1) what is the relationship between EEA and gender differences; (2) what is the relationship between the EEA and the Broad-Based Black Economic Empowerment (BBBEE) initiatives; (3) what has been the impact of the EEA on organisational change; (4) what have been the main impacts since the implementation of the EEA?

This type of research enabled the researcher to contribute to the current body of knowledge, influence policy, qualitatively identify current EEA gaps, and quantify the plausibility of the results through numbers, statistical analyses, and graphs.

The findings suggest that the South African Government, through the Department of Employment and Labour needs to look at the impact of the EEA on the broader workforce, especially entities that are regarded as designated employers. Areas of impact should focus on gender, empowerment and change management within these organisations.

Keywords: Broad-Based Black Economic Empowerment, employment equity, gender, change, designated employers

1. Introduction

1.1. Definition of Employment Equity

The Employment Equity Act No. 55 of 1998 (EEA) was introduced by the South African government to address the legacy of apartheid and ensure equitable representation of black people and women in the South African labour market. Although the impacts of the Act are highly controversial, its widespread adoption among firms opens up questions on its impact on the structure of the South African labour market. The purpose of the EEA is to achieve equity in the workplace by promoting equal opportunity and fair treatment in employment through elimination of unfair discrimination and implementing affirmative action measures to redress the disadvantages in employment experienced by designated groups, where EEA applies to all employers and workers and protects workers and job seekers from unfair discrimination, and also provides a framework for implementing affirmative action.

Adjusted Recognition for Gender (ARG) will recognize employers with progressive Black women representation in a measurement category. The 2006-2007 DTI alignment process preserved the employment equity foundation and encouraged employers to implement it more vigorously, which pleased the Commission.

The beneficiaries of affirmative action, also known as **designated employers**, are limited to black people (i.e. Africans, Coloured's and Indians), women and people with disabilities who are citizens of the Republic of South Africa by birth or descent https://www.vut.ac.za/social-justice-and-transformation-employment-equity-report/ , accessed on 2 May 2023, (Vaal University of Technology, 2022). Twenty-four years of the EEA, inequity still thrives in the South African workplace. More than two decades since the enactment of the EEA to transform the South African labour market compliance levels still remain regretfully low (MENA Report, 2022).

This study primarily focuses on answering the following: the relationship between EEA and gender differences; the relationship between the EEA and the Broad-Based Black Economic Empowerment (BBBEE) initiatives; the impact of the EEA on organisational change; and the main impacts since the implementation of the EEA.

In response to the above variables, we narrowly focused on the role of **designated employers** as defined by the Labour Department of the Republic of South Africa, (2022: 01) as *" an employer who employs 50 or more employees, or an employer who* *employs fewer than 50 employees, but has a total annual turnover as reflected in Schedule 4 of the Act; municipalities and organs of State. Employers can also volunteer to become designated employers."*

Table 1 Schedule four (4) of the EEA

Sector or subsectors in accordance with the Standard Industrial Classification	***Total annual turnover* (Old)**	***Total annual turnover* (New)**
Agriculture	R 2,00m	R6,00 m
Mining and Quarrying	R 7,50m	R22,50 m
Manufacturing	R10,00m	R30,00 m
Electricity, Gas and Water	R10,00m	R30,00 m
Construction	R 5,00m	R15,00 m
Retail and Motor Trade and Repair Services	R15,00m	R45,00 m
Wholesale Trade, Commercial Agents and Allied Services	R25,00m	R75,00 m
Catering, Accommodation and other Trade	R 5,00m	R15,00 m
Transport, Storage and Communications	R10,00m	R30,00 m
Finance and Business Services	R10,00m	R30,00 m
Community, Special and Personal Services	R 5,00m	R15,00 m

A designated employer has the responsibility to ensure that the EEA us implemented and must prepare a plan to achieve employment equity, which must:

1) have objectives for each year of the plan;
2) include affirmative action measures;
3) have numerical goals for achieving equitable representation;
4) have a timetable for each year;
5) have internal monitoring and evaluation procedures, including internal dispute resolution mechanisms, and
6) identify persons, including senior managers, to monitor and implement the plan.

1.2. Importance of Employment Equity in South Africa

Research conducted by Oosthuizen & Naidoo, (2010: 02) gives an indication that the South African employees' post-apartheid employment equity experiences enriches post-apartheid EE debates. These debates are normally along the lines of race, gender, age, and historical discrimination. Democratic principles like the EEA and diversity, require policy and practice changes, coupled with Affirmative Action (AA) programs, and the Broad Based Black Economic Empowerment (BBBEE) legislation that we will elaborate on later in this paper, have the main aim of addressing racial inequalities.

In South Africa, the Broad-Based Black Economic Empowerment (B-BBEE) Act is a crucial piece of legislation that seeks to correct the economic imbalances caused by apartheid. This conduct is not only necessary but essential for the country's genuine social and economic transformation. By instituting B-BBEE, South Africa can ensure that previously disadvantaged individuals have equal access to economic opportunities, allowing them to actively participate in various economic sectors and contribute to the development of the economy.

One of the most compelling reasons to support the B-BBEE Act is that it promotes diversity and inclusivity in the business sector. This act creates a more equitable playing field where everyone has an equal opportunity to succeed by providing preferential treatment to historically disadvantaged groups, such as black Africans, Coloureds, and Indians. This not only promotes a sense of equity and equality, but also innovation and creativity by incorporating multiple perspectives into decision-making processes.

Furthermore, the implementation of B-BBEE results in long-term economic benefits for the entire nation. When formerly marginalised groups are economically empowered, they become active contributors to society rather than reliant on government support alone. This leads to increased employment creation, higher household incomes, and a reduction in poverty. Moreover, encouraging entrepreneurship in these communities stimulates economic development through the creation of new enterprises and investments.

Lastly, the Broad-Based Black Economic Empowerment Act is a necessary instrument for redressing past injustices and establishing a genuinely inclusive economy in South Africa. By granting historically marginalised groups access to economic opportunities, this act ensures equitable competition, promotes diversity, and stimulates sustainable economic development for the benefit of all citizens.

The thrust of the EEA is to promote equal employment and representation for designated groups in South Africa through AA. Addressing employment equity (EE) appointment imbalances allows new business streams and protects minorities, while addressing negative beliefs and self-affirmation tasks improves effectiveness. EE, AA, and BBBEE can reduce racial inequality, but employees fear tokenism, marginalization, and retribution. Legislation and organizational practices reward skilled workers, but implementation and communication issues persist, prompting debate and possible EEA abolition. Reverse discrimination, lack of training, and victimization hinder employment equity and affirmative action implementation and postcolonial struggles. Employment equity experiences show that black male and female participants value equal opportunities and work relations, while white participants suffer from stereotypes and discrimination.

According to a case study conducted by Utete, (2022: 143 - 145) in a leading South African organisation, showed that employee performance research is scarce, but developing countries with skill shortages need employment equity in order to reduce discrimination and boost productivity, determination, and ability, improving employee performance and organisational success. To give designated groups equal opportunities, organisations must follow non-discrimination and affirmative action laws. South Africa's EEA promotes disability equality and representation, but employment equity legislation is resisted by apathy and fear of displacement. White-male-dominated organisational culture, inconsistent implementation, lack of shared understanding, and poor communication are some of the critical issues to be addressed.

1.3. Overview of the history of Employment Equity in South Africa

South Africa's EEA, which selectively focuses on affirmative action and past imbalances, raises concerns about affirmative action undermining merit, corruption, and industrial relations.

Corruption

Rousseau once asserted that the legitimacy of national public power derives from the people, as cited by Liu, (2016). The government is the sovereign's executor and its authority is derived from the trust of the people. When the use of public authority deviates from its intended course and is abused, corruption issues arise. It fits the definition of "the misuse of public office for personal gain." This definition is also the one most frequently used by international scholars to describe corruption.

Industrial relations

The research conducted by Fashoyin (1998) revealed the irony of the extensive and generally positive reformation of industrial relations in South Africa, especially in terms of the policy framework. The author argues that similar institutions in other countries negatively impacted by these reforms have yet to completely surmount the problem of legitimacy, internal vulnerability, and what appears to be an indeterminate trajectory of public policy. Therefore, it should not be surprised for the observer that the practise of labour relations in Southern Africa is highly adversarial. This appears to be the legacy of apartheid in countries like Namibia and South Africa.

In this regard, the ILO's primary responsibility was to guarantee the advancement of industrial relations in Southern Africa by assisting constituents in implementing the positive regional initiatives. It also includes assisting to strengthen and promote the process of reforms intended at institutionalising social protection, by strengthening tripartite consultation on social and economic decision making, for instance.

The South Africa's 1994 Human Rights Act promotes labour equity and affirmative action for blacks, women, and disabled people in the understanding apartheid's effects on group classification, rights, and self-determination which are essential to understanding labour equity in South Africa. South Africa's racially segregated labour market necessitated strict measures to achieve equality, therefore the introduction of the EEA. The 1999 Employment Equity Act aim is to combat discrimination and promoted diversity, gender equality, but patriarchal attitudes, cultural views, and male employees' resistance kept male managers favouring men. Organisational glass ceilings limit women's career advancement.

Equal Employment Opportunity (EEO) and AA laws aim to end gender discrimination and give women equal opportunities. To combat gender inequality in the workplace, South Africa implemented EEO and affirmative action.

Diversity management seeks equal employment, where South African affirmative action has increased black enrolment but does not provide employment, education, or income benefits for the needy. It empowers politically, not economically. Despite concerns about affirmative action's fairness and implementation, the EEA of 1998 promotes workplace equality. Political elites may use the EEA to promote corruption and nepotism, hurting the poorest designated groups (Nzima & Duma, 2014).

The EEA since its inception in 1998 may have caused employment distortion, inefficient resource allocation, and lower labour employment, especially at small and medium enterprises, indicating its counterproductive effect (Bophelo Mtezuka, 2017). Economic reforms, job creation, and worker rights followed South Africa's 1994 democratic elections, addressing inequality and inclusive labour markets. Legislative prescripts like the Labour Relations Act (LRA), Basic Condition of Employment Act (BCEA), and EE raise labour costs for smaller firms and global market competitors.

South Africa's EEA empowered Black workers, but implementation is difficult in promoting equality, eliminating unfair discrimination, ensuring employment equity, achieving a diverse workforce, promoting economic development, and fulfilling the International Labour Organisation (ILO) obligations (Flowerday et al., 2016).

1.4. Findings on the Literature

This section highlights some of the main issues uncovered through the literature. The Employment Equity Act No. 55 of 1998 aims to promote equal representation of blacks and women in the South African labour market. However, workplace inequality persists despite 24 years of EEA implementation. The EEA's focus on affirmative action raises concerns about tokenism, marginalization, and retaliation. The ILO's responsibility is to advance industrial relations in Southern Africa. Promoting equality, eradicating unjust discrimination, ensuring employment equity, attaining a diverse workforce, promoting economic development, and meeting ILO’s obligations are challenging to implement.

2. Methodology

We have made use of an analytical and systematic review process by synthesising secondary data through the use of repeatable analytical methods. We created the research questions in order to find and synthesise relevant data, and present an exhaustive review of current evidence. We used the mixed methods design (Creswell, 2012) and collected both quantitative and qualitative data.

The mixed methods design is based on the idea that combining quantitative and qualitative data improves research problem understanding. Mixed methods designs collect, analyse, and mix quantitative and qualitative data in a single study or multiphase series of studies.

In this process, we decided on giving priority to each type of data, which type we will collect first (concurrent or sequential), how the data will be "mixed" the data (integrating or connecting), and whether we will use theory to guide the study (e.g., advocacy or social science theory).

In performing our systematic review we followed these steps: (1) defining the four research questions, searching for relevant data sources (website searches) , (2) extracting data from the South African Employment Equity Commission Annual Reports from 1999 – 2022, synthetise and summarised the data in tables, (3) evaluated the data and (4) provided a conclusion. Data was extracted, assessed for eligibility, analysed, and combined for a complete result (Nunn & Chang, 2020).

Systematic reviews synthesize data more thoroughly and makes use of both quantitative and qualitative research methods, clear objectives, reproducible methodology, systematic search, validity assessment, and systematic presentation of findings. In this systematic review paper we include a brief literature review, research question, methodology, search procedures, eligibility criteria, data extraction, data synthesis, and a conclusion (Clarke, 2011).

3. The early stages of employment equity in South Africa (1998 - 2003)

3.1. The introduction of affirmative action policies

In 1994, South Africa gained democracy and abolished Apartheid . The EEA was the most significant law to correct past injustices. The EEA promotes equality, eliminates unfair labour practices, and implements affirmative action (AA) to compensate designated groups for past disadvantages. Blacks, women, and disabled people still struggled in the job market, mostly due to apartheid-era education standards and quality.

The introduction of South Africa's affirmative action policies in 1998 aim to address inequality, racial segregation and discrimination by giving minorities equal opportunities. Affirmative action in South Africa ensures "Black People" receive equal benefits and opportunities, reducing unemployment. After the abolishment of the apartheid system, affirmative action in South Africa promoted quality skills development, honest dialogue, and government intervention to fight poverty and spread knowledge.

Due to patriarchal dominance, South African women face career barriers, and affirmative action is criticized for negative stereotyping, stigmatization, lack of oversight, and potential reverse discrimination. Due to reverse discrimination, resistance, and backlash, some perceptions exist that compares affirmative action to apartheid, highlighting its paradoxical effects (Archibong et al., 2013).

The EEA was introduced in South Africa to address employment inequality and other related issues, but the objective of addressing inequality has not been met.

The term Affirmative Action (AA) as articulated under chapter 2 of the EEA IS used to describe actions to prevent discrimination and enhance opportunities for designated groups who had been previously discriminated against on the basis of their race, gender, sexual orientation, age, etc.(Bophelo Mtezuka, 2017).

EE and AA are both legislatively driven and aim to address workplace inequalities based on race, gender, and disability; thus, EE and AA are necessary to correct past injustices and diversify South Africa's public and private sectors. EE and AA are related concepts, so this study uses them interchangeably (Omar & Kiley, 2022).

3.2. The establishment of the Employment Equity Commission

Section 30 of the Employment Equity Act, 1998 (EEA) established the Commission for Employment Equity. The commission advises the minister on: section 54's code of good practice; section 55's regulations; and this act's policy and other matters.

Section 54

Section 54 of the Employment Equity Act in South Africa is an essential provision that seeks to promote equitable employment opportunities and reasonable workplace representation. This section mandates that designated employers conduct regular pay audits to identify and correct any unjust discrimination in compensation practises. It plays a crucial role in addressing the pervasive gender pay disparity and ensuring that employees are compensated equitably based on their skills, qualifications, and experience as opposed to their gender.

South Africa can strive towards a more inclusive and equitable society by implementing Section 54. The provision encourages employers to examine their compensation structures critically and eliminate any discriminatory practises. This not only benefits individual employees but also contributes to the development of a more robust workforce by promoting diversity and equity. Moreover, this provision conveys a clear message that unequal pay will not be tolerated in the South African society, thereby nurturing an atmosphere in which all individuals have the opportunity to succeed professionally without confronting superfluous barriers based on their gender or any other protected characteristic. Hence, Section 54 of the Employment Equity Act is an essential instrument for promoting equality and equity in the workplace, and its implementation should be supported by all parties engaged in defining the employment landscape in South Africa (Nxesi, 2022).

Section 55

This section makes provision for the Minister of Employment and Labour to publish regulations in the government gazette, that deals inter alia with the following:

(1) The Minister may on the advice of the Commission, make any regulation regarding

a) any matter that this Act requires or permits to be prescribed: and
b) any administrative or procedural matters that may be necessary or expedient to achieve the proper and effective administration of the Act

(2) The Minister may by notice in the Gazette make a regulation providing for separate and simplified forms and procedures in respect of the obligations created by sections 19, 20, 21, 25 and 26 for employers that employ fewer than 150 employees (Department of Labour, 2014).

In addition to the functions in subsection (1), the Commission may: (1) make awards for employers who advance this Act; (2) research and report to the Minister on any matter relating to the application of this Act, including appropriate and well-researched norms and benchmarks for numerical goals in various sectors; and (3) perform any other prescribed function. https://www.labour.gov.za/About-Us/Pages/CEE.aspx, accessed on 15 May 2023 (Government of South Africa, 1998).

3.3. Employment Equity (1998 – 2003) – Early stages timelines

3.3.1. EEA and Gender

Parliament's 1998 Employment Equity Act (EEA) addressed South Africa's economic and social inequality. The EEA was introduced during extreme labour market disparities by race, gender, and disability. Human resource development became necessary for employment equity after 1998–2003 where workplace discrimination underutilized a large portion of the productive population, hurting economic growth and global competitiveness. It became necessary to compare EEA and Economically Active Population (EAP) workforces by occupational category, level, race, gender, and disability (CEE, 2002).

During the 2002 – 2003 report we noticed some developments in terms of the gender parities, for example the poor representation of Black females among the total representation of Blacks and the total representation of females which suggested that inadequate attention is being paid to the compounded disadvantage due to the intersection between race and gender. (Chief Directorate of Communication Department of Labour, 2002) This is more displayed by the table below.

Table 2 Changes at Top Management Level (2000 – 2002)

Top Management 2000	Top Management 2002	% Change
Gender	*Gender*	*Gender*
• Females accounted for 12.4%	• Females accounted for 13.7%	• 1.3%
• Males accounted for 87.6%	• Males accounted for 86.2%	• -1.4%
• African females accounted for 1.2%	• African females accounted for 2.0%	• 0.8%
• Coloured females accounted for 0.7%	• Coloured females accounted for 0.7%	• 0.0%
• Indian females accounted for 0.5%	• Indian females accounted for 0.6%	• 0.1%
• White females accounted for 10.2%	• White females accounted for 10.4%	• 0.2%
• African males accounted for 5.0%	• African males accounted for 8.0%	• 3.0%
• Coloured males accounted for 2.0%	• Coloured males accounted for 2.7%	• 0.7%
• Indian males accounted for 3.3%	• Indian males accounted for 4.4%	• 1.1%
• White males accounted for 77.3%	• White males accounted for 71.1%	• -6.2%
[1]The table shows that female representation in all top management positions increased by 1.3%. African female representation increased from 1.2 % in 2000 to 2.0% in 2002; Coloured female representation remained at 0.7% in both 2000 and 2002; Indian female representation increased from 0.5% in 2000 to 0.6% in 2002; and White female representation changed from 10.2% in 2000 to 10.4% in 2002. It is interesting to note that although Black representation increased by 5.7% in positions at this level, the benefits associated with this increase accrued mainly to Black males (4.8%).		

3.3.2. EEA and BBBEE

The Broad-Based Black Economic Empowerment Act 53 of 2003 seeks economic equality for black and white South Africans. The B-BBEEA aims to addresses apartheid-era racial imbalances to empower black South Africans. The B-BBEEA evaluates meaningful ownership, skills and management development, rural development, black female empowerment, and job creation, as well as fronting practices and legislative efforts.

[1] Adopted from Commission for Employment Equity Annual Report 2002 - 2003

BEE promotes economic equality for black people, whilst the Procurement Policy Act favour historically disadvantaged suppliers. The B-BBEEA addresses race in ownership, management, and skilled occupations to empower blacks.

Whites have lost senior management positions since 2003, while Africans have increased but remain underrepresented and management remains racially mixed. The B-BBEEA showed from 2003 a decline in white, African, Coloured, and Indian skilled technical occupations, with fronting practices hindering goals. The B-BBEEA defines fronting as faking BEE compliance.

These practices can cause fraud and hinder goals. The B-BBEEA governs black economic empowerment. BEE is "*a specific government policy to advance economic transformation and enhance economic participation of black people in the South African economy.*" (van de Rheede, 2020).

3.3.3. EEA and Organisational Changes

The workforce race and gender conclusions were based on available data for the reporting period of 1999 - 2001. Not all targeted companies reported during this period, whilst some reports did not follow the rules, so their data was not included in the 1999 – 2001 Commission of Employment Equity report sample. This implied that the next reports may change due to new information rather than workplace changes.

The 2002 – 2003 report from the Commission welcomed stakeholder suggestions on innovative ways to accelerate workplace change through the EEA and related legislation. Furthermore, a National Study into the Implementation of the EEA in the Private Sector in South Africa, 2000-2002, was commissioned by the Commission to examine private sector implementation of the Act. The study sampled 67 private sector employers proportionally from each of the nine provinces based on economic activity.

The results showed that general compliance patterns are good on paper but poor when workplace change is considered. Further results showed that stakeholder participation is low, objectives and goal setting are poorly executed, and no formal policies or programs address racism, sexism, and disability discrimination.

Companies lack commitment to employment equity processes, leadership, and internal capacity to implement change, and low-level input from organized labour is a serious issue (Chief Directorate of Communication Department of Labour, 2002).

3.3.4. *EEA Impacts on implementation*

The Commission on Employment Equity report was during the inception phases from 1999 – 2001 and could not report on any significant impact during this implementation period.

During the 2002 – 2003 reporting period though, the commission visited private and public employers to assess their implementation of the Act, particularly in eradicating unfair discrimination and meeting affirmative action targets.

A study was conducted to examine private sector Act implementation. The report's data was extrapolated from employer reports and the Labour Force Survey's Economically Active Population (LFSEAP), which included Blacks (Africans, Coloureds, and Indians) who remained underrepresented in key positions in the workforce, according to the analysis. The Parliamentary Portfolio Committee on Labour, during this period of 2002 - 2003 held public hearings to assess and track the EEA implementation. The Commission used these events to share its experiences and hear others' concerns and challenges. Instead of changing laws, it advised adding mechanisms to improve implementation and monitoring.

To bring defaulters to the Labour Court and increase and improve enforcement processes (Chief Directorate of Communication Department of Labour, 2002).

This section highlights that the goals set by the South African government of combating inequality has not been achieved. Affirmative action (AA) is employed to prevent discrimination and increase opportunities for designated groups on the basis of race, gender, sexual orientation, and age.

By instituting Section 54, which encourages employers to critically examine their compensation structures and eliminate discriminatory practises, South Africa can work towards a more inclusive and equitable society.

The Broad-Based Black Economic Empowerment Act 53 of 2003 on the other hand seeks economic equality for black and white South Africans, addressing apartheid-era racial disparities and promoting economic equality for black individuals. However, fronting practises impede reaching some critical objectives and making some significant progress.

The Commission's 2002-2003 report invited stakeholder suggestions on innovative methods to accelerate workplace change via the EEA and related legislation. The research uncovered poor compliance patterns in workplace change, minimal stakeholder participation, and ineffective execution of objectives and goal formulation. Companies lack commitment to employment equity processes, lack of internal capacity, and concerted leadership. The Commission on Employment Equity recommended the addition of mechanisms for enhanced implementation and monitoring, the referral of defaulters to the Labour Court, and the expansion of enforcement processes.

4. The development of employment equity in South Africa (2004 - 2013)

4.1. The amendments to the Employment Equity Act in 2013

The National Assembly passed the Employment Equity Amendment Act 47 of 2013 on 24 October 2013 and the President signed it on 14 January 2014 (Republic of South Africa, 2014). The Act sought to strengthens enforcement of the EEA taking into consideration the systemic challenges from 1999 – 2013, and prohibits workplace discrimination. It seek equality, fairness, employment equity, and a diverse workforce. The amended Act limited AA only to South African citizens, banned arbitrary discrimination, and allowed employers publish a code of good practice for assessing equal-value work. Disputes on sexual harassment, underpayment, or consent, could then be referred to the Commission for Conciliation, Mediation and Arbitration (CCMA) and appealed to the Labour Court.

Through the amendment of the EEA in 2013, employers are compelled to prove that discrimination was not rational, justifiable, or justified. Reports, valid reasons, and employment equity plans must be submitted to avoid fines.

The EEA prohibited workplace discrimination and strengthened enforcement.

The Minister may issue regulations to ensure employers train qualified designated group members. Increased fines should go to the National Revenue Fund. Designated employers must report employment equity plans to the Department of Labour.

4.2. The introduction of the Broad Based Black Economic Empowerment Act

The Broad-Based Black Economic Empowerment Act (BBBEE) was introduced in South Africa in 2003 as a means to redress the economic inequalities that had existed since apartheid. The legislation aimed to ensure that black South Africans, who were previously marginalized and excluded from the mainstream economy, would have access to opportunities for growth and development.

The BBBEE act is intended to promote economic transformation by empowering black people in all sectors of society, including business, government, and civil society. The introduction of the BBBEE Act was a landmark event in South African history. It signalled the commitment of the government and private sector to address the legacy of apartheid by creating a more inclusive and equitable society. Since its implementation, there has been significant progress towards achieving economic empowerment for black South Africans.

However, there are still challenges that need to be addressed, such as ensuring that the benefits of empowerment reach those who need it most. Nevertheless, the BBBEE act remains an important tool for promoting social justice and inclusive economic growth in South Africa. The study conducted by van de Rheede, (2020) and published in 2020 on the impact of the B-BBEA of 2003 indicated the failure to promote racial diversity in skilled technical occupations. Fronting has decreased white, coloured, and Indian people and increased African people, affecting this goal. The slow rate of racial composition changed in enterprise ownership and management structures and skilled occupations has slowed progress. Since 2016, the Act requires government, public entities, and financial transactions with public entities to comply. The B-BBEECom has a mandate to resolve complaints and contraventions and may investigate BEE fronting complaints.

The B-BBEE Com can sue for fronting and other BBBEEA violations and can refer criminal investigations to the appropriate division and report illegal or regulated behaviour to the South African Revenue Service or regulators. The B-BBEEA criminalizes fronting and providing false information to BEE verification professionals assessing an enterprise's BEE status. Procurement officers, both within the public and private sectors and verification agencies can be sanctioned. Non-natural persons face fines, imprisonment, and fines for violations, where heavy penalties are commendable (van de Rheede, 2020).

4.3. [2]The progress made in achieving Employment Equity targets

The table below gives an indication of the achievement of Employment Equity targets from the 2001 – 2013 financial years. This form part of the methodology applied in analysing the submitted reports.

[2] Data collected and summarised from the Commission on Employment Equity Annual Reports from 2001 - 2013

Table 3 – Employment Equity targets (2003 – 2004)

Population group	Economically active			EE 2003		
	Male	**Female**	**Total**	**Male**	**Female**	**Total**
African	6 307 537	5 649 317	11 956 854	1 220 153	526 753	1 746 906
	38.6%	34.5%	73.1%	41.5%	17.9%	59.4%
Coloured	918 271	853 202	1 771 473	190 617	183 413	374 030
	5.6%	5.2%	10.8%	6.5%	6.2%	12.7%
Indian	345 124	223 868	568 992	84 747	61 146	145 893
	2.1%	1.4%	3.5%	2.9%	2.1%	5.0%
White	1 153 648	910 415	2 064 062	387 276	286 893	674 169
	7.0%	5.6%	12.6%	13.2%	9.8%	22.9%
Total	**8 724 579**	**7 636 802**	**16 361 381**	**1 882 793**	**1 058 205**	**2 940 998**
	53.3%	**46.7%**	**100%**	**64%**	**36.0%**	**100%**

Figure 1 – Employment Equity targets (2003 – 2004)

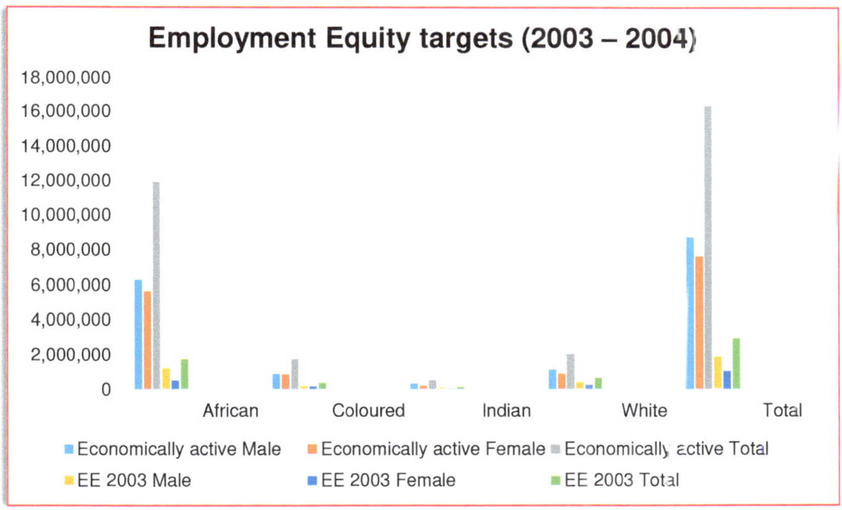

Table 4 – EE Reports from 2001 – 2013

Year	Reports received	Reports excluded	Reports included in analysis	% Reports for analysis
2001	2 369	587	1 782	75.2%
2002	6 990	0	6 990	100%
2003	3 252	0	3 252	100.0%
2004	5 554	0	5 554	100%
2005	2 762	677	2 085	75.5%
2006	6 876	2 482	4 394	63.9%
2007	2 858	1 365	1 493	52.2%
2008	10 580	3 351	7 229	68.3%
2009	3 695	326	3 369	91.2%
2010	18 534	1 836	16 698	90.1%
2011	4 492	122	4 370	97.3%
2012	23 312	1 300	22 012	94.4%
2013	5102	118	4984	97.7%

Figure 2 – EEA reports received and analysed (2001 – 2013)

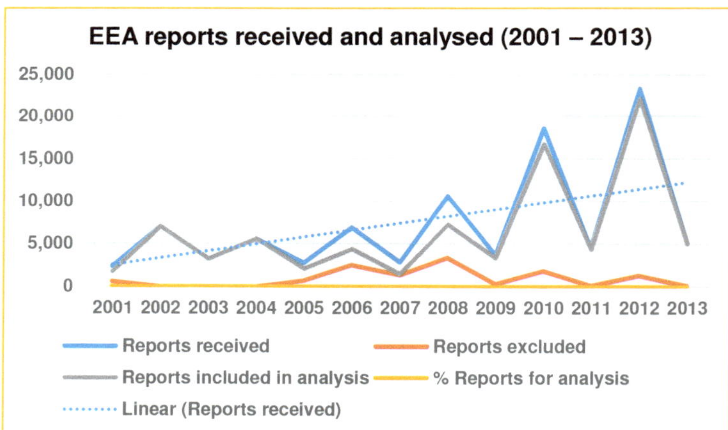

The above tables and figures bear reference to the information below.

The 2004–2013 annual reports compare employment equity demographics to the economically active population. The economically active population is 87.4% Black, 12.6% White, 46.7% female, 53.3% male. In 2003, Blacks were 77.1%, Whites 22.9%, females 36.0%, and males 64.0%.

The 2005-2006 CEE report still analyses employment equity targets, despite format changes. In 2000, 2002, and 2004, large and small employers reported employment equity. In 2001, 369 reports were received and 1,782 were analysed, in 2003, 325 and 3,252, and in 2005, 2,762 and 2,085.

Large employers reported 37.2% more from 2001 to 2003 but 15% less from 2003 to 2005. This decrease was identified, so improvements are needed. From 2001 to 2005, top management, senior management, and professionals had disappointing representation. South Africa needs to transform its economy, but workplace employment equity implementation is slow and uneven.

Broad-Based Black Economic Empowerment (BBEE) surveys on economic transformation raise this concern. Employment equity and BBBEE failures require compliance changes. Black top management representation rose 2.1% from 25.1% in 2001 to 27.2% in 2005, while African representation rose from 8.0% to 17.91%. Top management female representation rose 4.6% from 11.9% in 2001 to 16.5% in 2005, with African female representation rising from 1.6% to 3.1%. The EAP has almost twice as many white women.

The 2006-2007 annual report analysis sought to balance the employment equity scorecard after employers made slow progress since the Employment Equity Act of 1998.

The Employment Equity Scorecard (EES) rewards employers with at least 40% Black employee representation. Employers who meet or exceed the Black Economically Active Population (EAP) percentage for each measurement category receive bonus points. The reported statistics showed that Africans (74.1%) are in the majority, followed by Whites (12.8%), Coloureds (8.9%), and Indians (2.5%) respectively. EAP trails the National Population Distribution (NPD) only for Africans, while all Whites are economically active. Section 54 requires all levels and categories to reflect the EAP and represent race and gender equally. The 2007-2008 annual report continued the 2006-2007 trends, but reinstated EEA Sections 43, 44, and 45. Twenty-six (26)

Johannesburg Stock Exchange (JSE) listed companies were reviewed for EEA violations during the 2007 – 2008 financial year.

Without consulting employees, analysing workplaces, or creating an employment equity plan with annual goals, these companies submitted reports to the Department of Labour. All 26 employers violated the law by not considering the Employment Equity Plan (EAP) and setting ambitious annual numerical targets. Most of these employers did not hire disabled people or manage HIV/AIDS in the workplace. The BBBEE scorecard on employment equity showed that 79.0% of South Africans are Africans, followed by Whites, Coloureds, and Indians. South Africa's EAP stood at 74.8 percent African.

The 2008-2009 annual report analysed employment equity trends for 2004-2008, including large and small employers, and 2003, 2005, and 2007, were the three most important reporting periods for large employers. From 2004 to 2006, employment equity reports and employees decreased. Mergers, closures/liquidations, consolidations, and status changes increased reports and employees from 2006 to 2008. In 2008, 1,000% more employers reported online through the Commission's system.

The 2009-2010 annual report analysis highlighted systemic challenges and recommended that the Minister engage government and businesses to improve disability representation, engage the BEE Council on employment equity matters, promote fair remuneration, amend regulations, review the Code of Good Practice on HIV and AIDS in the workplace, and develop a process to make EE certification a tendering condition. The EAP and National Demographics by race and gender, which is used to set employment equity numerical goals and targets are used throughout this paper.

From 2001 to 2010, the CEE compared large and small employers' employment equity reports. After 10 years, whites still dominated most occupations, with employers hiring and promoting mostly whites at middle-to-upper levels.

Affirmative action benefited white women more than African, Coloured, and disabled women. Employers hired and promoted more men than women proportionally to population size (EAP). Whites dominated high-earning occupations and Blacks have fewer training opportunities, hurting employment equity.

Due to slow change and employer reluctance, the CEE recommended amending the EEA to improve implementation and enforcement. Despite good BBBEE ratings, companies still performed poorly on EE, misrepresenting transformation. EAP and other data can help employers set employment equity numerical goals and targets.

Employers use the EEA to allocate resources and implement interventions for a diverse workforce. Employers have submitted more and more accurate reports since tightened regulations. Online submissions increased report accuracy by over 90% in 2011, analysing 97.3% of 4 492 reports. Late in 2010, the EEA was reviewed and amended to allow enough implementation time before closing administrative and technical gaps in the legislation. The Employment Equity Bill proposed redefining "designated groups" to guarantee affirmative action for South African citizens born before 27 April 1994 and their descendants. The International Labour Organization (ILO) has called for a race and gender wage discrimination provision to address unfair employer discrimination in employment terms and conditions. Simplifying the EE Act's enforcement provisions will improve enforcement and prevent tactical use of written undertakings, compliance orders, and DG general reviews.

The proposed amendments also allowed the DG to apply to the Labour Court to fine an employer for failing to comply with a request or recommendation made during a review of Act compliance. The CEE and DTI aligned employment equity and BBBEE in March 2013 through public hearings to amend the BBBEE and its Codes. A clear definition and alignment of Black people and transformation legislation and policies beneficiaries, a "trumping clause" to ensure the BBBBEA supersedes any other Act, Code, or Charter for BBBEE-specific matters, mandatory provisions for the State to apply the BBBEE Codes, a strong and effective BBBEE Commission, concerns about the "Sectoral Charter" and "Sectoral Codes" approach, and concerns about truncating the EE elements.

Recruitment, promotion, and skills development patterns from 2002 to 2013 were alarming. However, the data showed causation. White males received 47.7% of senior management skills development and 47.4% of top management recruitment in 2012. Africans, Coloureds, and Indians received 14.8%, 3.7%, and 5.6%, respectively, whilst 5.6% of 2012 top managers were Indian. White females outnumbered Black males (12.6%) in top management and received more top management skills development than African males, African females, Coloured males, Coloured females, Indian males, and Indian females.

White males (42.6%) and Indian males (6.7%) were overrepresented in senior management. These recruitment trends and patterns are "throughput factors".

In 2012, white males (34.5%) had more senior management skills development than African males (16.8%) and were promoted into senior management more than any other group (32.1%). African senior managers were promoted 16.8%. Africans and women are promoted to senior management more due to the "deep hole" syndrome.

Since 2010-2012, Broad-Based Black Economic Empowerment and Employment Equity has shown this trend. BBBEE and EE amendments under Parliamentary review were well-timed and have not changed decision-making. Twenty (20) years of post-apartheid democracy and over 10 years of EE legislation have failed to change the approach and a call needed to be made to restore employment equity in order to progress. The 2013-2014 annual report identified issues like no senior and top leadership buy-in, junior staff assigned to EE managers, non-existent or improperly constituted consultative forums, and lack of consultation on EE plans.

Despite these challenges, employers received DG recommendations and sufficient time to implement them, and their EE Plans were monitored after DG approval. Positive strategies and practices have transformed employment equity. The Commission aligned the BBBEE and EEA regulations to key EEA as amended provisions, including their regulations. BBBEE beneficiaries now received affirmative action, and "designated groups" now include Black people, women, youth, people with disabilities, and rural residents who became citizens before 27 April 1994 or would have become citizens but for apartheid policies. The Act governs local governments, and EEA9 Annexure occupational levels matched BBBEE Codes. Code 200's Management and Control element now covers employment equity, reducing the BBBEE Codes' assessment elements from seven to five. Code 100 places Top Management under Ownership. Company turnover determines fines. Online submissions increased report accuracy by over 98%, and 97.7% of 5102 reports were analysed in the 2014–2015 annual report analysis. The Act considers employers who do not complete their reports to have not reported, increasing accuracy.

The 2014 EEA Regulations introduced the Employment Equity Reporting System, online submissions, and controls. Designated employers must report annually using simplified online forms under the 2014 Employment Equity Regulations. The regulations encourage information sharing and consultation and define criteria and methods for assessing equal-value work. They recommend classifying occupational levels using different job evaluation and grading systems. The EAP helps employers assess underrepresentation of designated groups and set numerical goals for an equitable and representative workforce.

Section 15 of the EEA requires employers to give suitably qualified people from designated groups equal employment opportunities and representation in all occupational levels. To promote equity, employers should use the EAP to hire qualified EE candidates, but education, training, and work experience can help achieve transformation goals.

Increasing economically active women is especially important when their population exceeds their EAP. EE reports rose 10.4% to 24 291 in 2014.

5. [3]The current state of employment equity in South Africa (2014 - 2022)

5.1. The challenges facing Employment Equity in South Africa

The tables and figures below are to be read with the narratives summaries in order to give an overview of the challenges facing EE in South Africa, mainly over the period of 2014 – 2022.

Table 5 – EEA reports received and analysed (2014 – 2015)

Provinces	**Reports received**	**Percentage**	**Employees**
Eastern Cape	1 342	5.5%	329 599
Free State	711	2.9%	168 947
Gauteng	11 181	46.0%	3 733 260
KwaZulu-Natal	3 320	13.7%	902 871
Limpopo	608	2.5%	238 085
Mpumalanga	1 410	5.8%	363 140
Northern Cape	306	1.3%	65 662
North West	592	2.4%	174 067
Western Cape	4 821	19.8%	1 043 250
TOTAL	**24 291**	**100.0%**	**7 018 881**

[3] Data collected and summarised from the Commission on Employment Equity Annual Reports from 2014 - 2022

Figure 3 – EEA reports received and analysed (2015 – 2016)

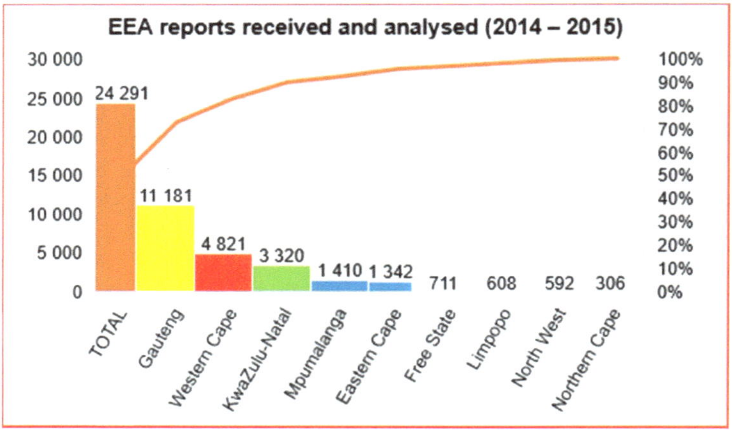

Table 6 – EEA reports received and analysed (2015 – 2016)

Provinces	**Reports received**	**Percentage**	**Employees**
Eastern Cape	1 345	5.4%	374 245
Free State	710	2.8%	145 925
Gauteng	11 492	45.9%	3 724 473
KwaZulu-Natal	3 455	13.8%	916 195
Limpopo	689	2.8%	238 253
Mpumalanga	1 454	5.8%	338 855
Northern Cape	327	1.3%	78 038
North West	631	2.5%	172 349
Western Cape	4 927	19.7%	1 098 807
TOTAL	**25 030**	**100.0%**	**7 087 140**

Figure 4 – EEA reports received and analysed (2015 – 2016)

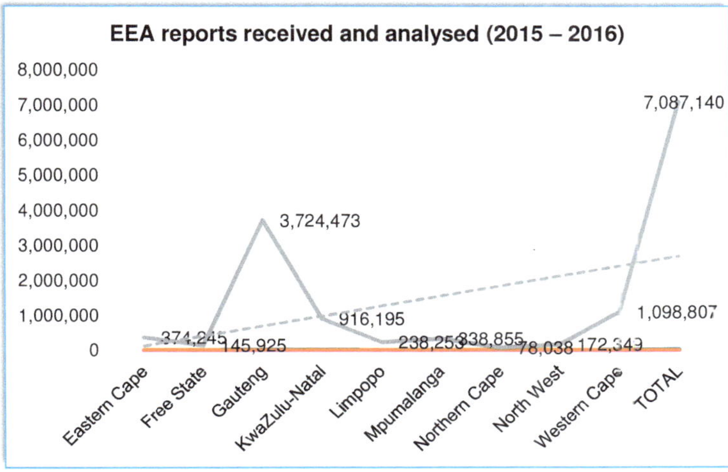

Table 7 – EEA reports received and analysed (2016 – 2017)

Provinces	**Reports received**	**Percentage**	**Employees**
Eastern Cape	1 384	5.3%	369 592
Free State	741	2.8%	146 963
Gauteng	11 810	45.0%	3 579 053
KwaZulu-Natal	3 768	14.4%	928 429
Limpopo	696	2.7%	238 012
Mpumalanga	1 501	5.7%	360 538
Northern Cape	362	1.4%	82 791
North West	640	2.4%	189 026
Western Cape	5 353	20.4%	1 177 045
TOTAL	**26 255**	**100.0%**	**7 071 449**

Figure 5 – EEA reports received and analysed (2016 – 2017)

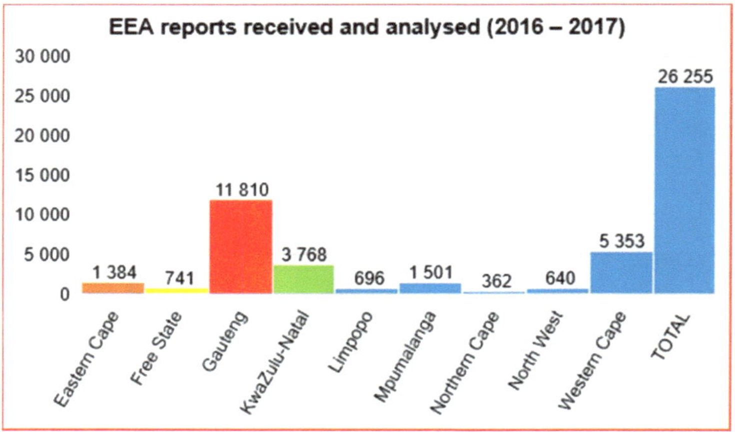

Table 8 – EEA reports received and analysed (2017 – 2018)

Provinces	Reports received	Percentage	Employees
Eastern Cape	1 440	5.3%	367 303
Free State	728	2.7%	151 848
Gauteng	12 165	44.8%	3 694 816
KwaZulu-Natal	4 029	14.8%	923 305
Limpopo	763	2.8%	257 638
Mpumalanga	1 491	5.5%	376 343
Northern Cape	381	1.4%	93 870
North West	646	2.4%	206 892
Western Cape	5 520	20.3%	1 227 413
TOTAL	**27 163**	**100.0%**	**7 299 428**

Figure 6 – EEA reports received and analysed (2017 – 2018)

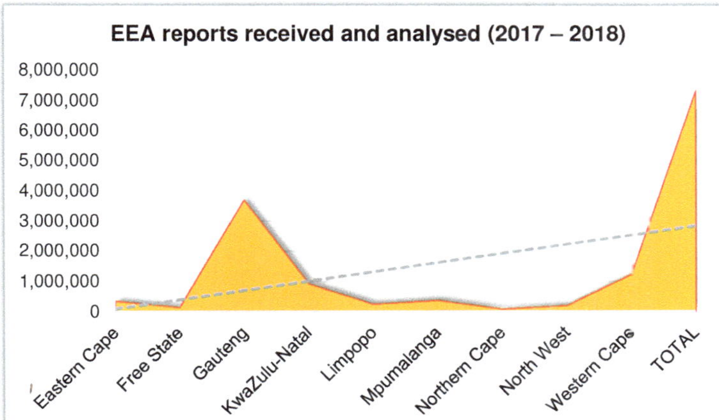

Table 9 – EEA reports received and analysed (2018 – 2019)

Provinces	Reports received	Percentage	Employees
Eastern Cape	1 426	5.2%	364 063
Free State	728	2.6%	148 270
Gauteng	12 090	44.0%	3 766 106
KwaZulu-Natal	4 156	15.1%	950 274
Limpopo	782	2.8%	266 824
Mpumalanga	1 528	5.6%	369 911
Northern Cape	673	2.4%	233 997
North West	385	1.4%	89 006
Western Cape	5 717	20.8%	1 227 425
TOTAL	**27 485**	**100.0%**	**7 415 876**

Figure 7 – EEA reports received and analysed (2018 – 2019)

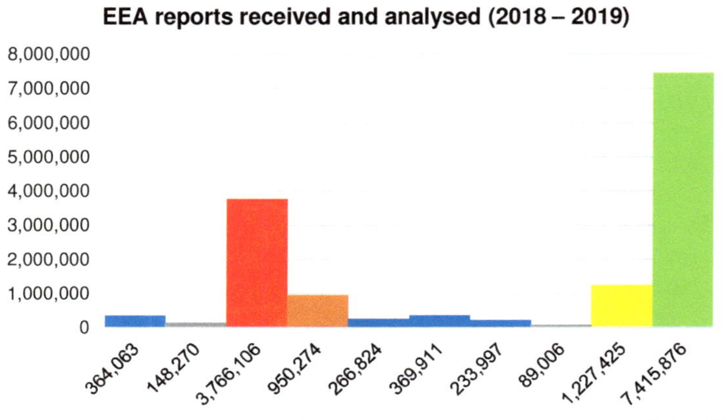

Table 10 – EEA reports received and analysed (2016 – 2021)

Reports received (all designated employers) from 2016 to 2021				
Year	**Reports received**	**Annual % Change**	**Employees covered**	**Annual % Change**
2016	26 255	Base	7 071 449	Base
2017	27 163	3.4%	7 299 428	4.9%
2018	27 485	1.2%	7 415 876	3.2%
2019	27 127	-1.3%	7 332 072	-1.1%
2020	26 635	-1.8%	7 056 059	-3.9%
2021	27 017	1.4%	7 079 355	0.3%

Figure 8 – EEA reports received and analysed (2016 – 2021)

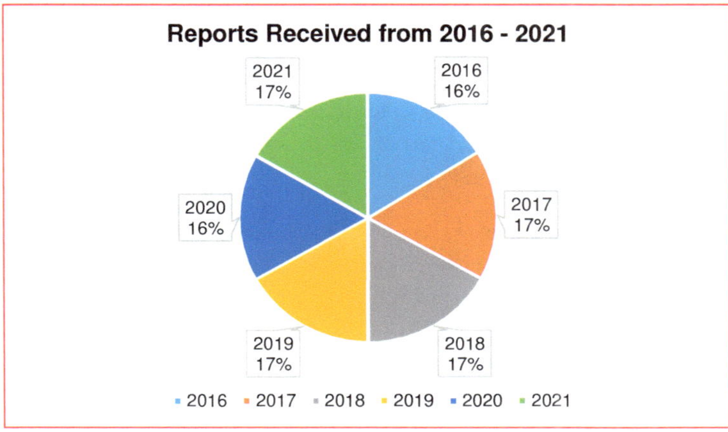

Figure 9 – EEA reports received and analysed (2016 – 2021)

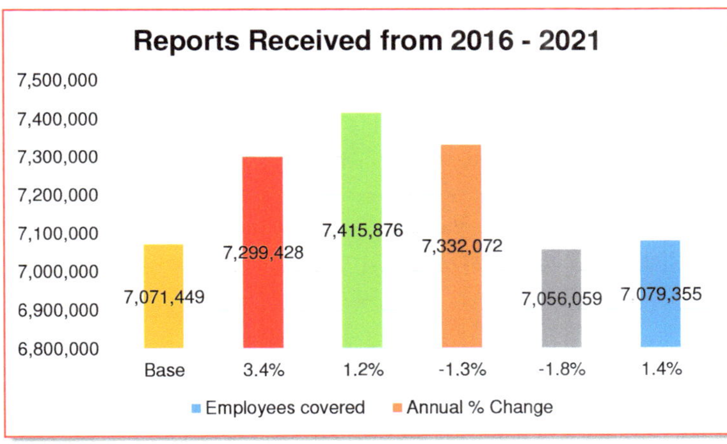

Figure 10 – Summary of Section 53 of the EEA

Section 53 of the EEA states that:

53. (1) Every employer that makes an offer to conclude an agreement with any organ of state for the furnishing of supplies or services to that organ of state or for the hiring or letting of anything.

(a) must-

(i) If it is a designated employer, comply with Chapter II and III of this Act, or

(ii) If it is not a designated employer, comply with Chapter II of this Act; and

(b) attach to that offer either-

(i) a certificate in terms of subsection (2) which is conclusive evidence that the employer complies with the relevant Chapters of this Act; or

(ii) a declaration by the employer that it complies with the relevant Chapters of this Act, which when verified by the Director-General, is conclusive evidence of compliance.

(2) An employer referred to in subsection (1) may request a certificate from the Minister confirming it compliance with Chapter II, or Chapters II and III, as the case may be.

(3) A certificate issued in terms of subsection (2) is valid for 12 months from the date of issue or until the next date on which the employer is obliged to submit a report in terms of section 21, whichever period is longer.

(4) A failure to comply with the relevant provisions of this Act is sufficient ground for rejection of any offer to conclude an agreement referred to in subsection (1) or for cancellation of the agreement.

(5) The Minister may in the code of good practice set out factors that must be taken into account by any person assessing whether an employer complies with Chapter II or Chapters II and III.

The 2015-2016 CEE Annual Report examined the government's strategic objectives for achieving fairness in employment by providing sound advice to the Minister of Labour on Employment Equity (EEA), engaging stakeholders to promote effective implementation, conducting research to inform and enrich the Commission's work, and monitoring and evaluating national employment equity trends.

EE report submissions increased by 3% in 2015. Gauteng employers reported 3.7 million employment equity reports, while Western Cape and KwaZulu-Natal reported 19.7% and 13.8%, respectively.

The reports cited that after 23 years of democracy and 21 years of the Constitution of the Republic of South Africa, social and economic inequalities, especially those from Colonialism, Apartheid, and Patriarchy, must be eliminated. These inequalities caused labour market discrimination against Black, Women, and Disabled people. Affirmative action and prohibiting unfair discrimination reinforce each other to achieve "substantive equality" to fulfill Section 9 of the Constitution. Legislation and other measures to help disadvantaged groups may promote equality. The EEA and other transformation laws implemented Constitutional Section 9 (2).

Section 9 (1) of the South African Constitution states that *"Everyone is equal before the law and has the right to equal protection and benefit of the law. (2) Equality includes the full and equal enjoyment of all rights and freedoms."*

Despite the 19-year EEA consolidation and comprehensive legal framework, transformation has been slow due to challenges like employer resistance to employment equity, not being recognised as a business imperative, and the lack of employment equity targets/benchmarks. The CEE Sectoral Engagements recommended Sectoral Employment Equity Targets as benchmarks and Section 53 of the EEA to accelerate transformation and compliance to ensure workplace equity.

Employment equity reports increased from 25,030 to 26,255 in 2016. Due to employer awareness of EEA compliance, EE reports rose 4.8% and 3.5 million Gauteng employees submitted 45.0 percent of these reports. Western Cape had 20.4% and KwaZulu-Natal 14.4%, respectively.

Section 15 of the EEA mandates affirmative action for designated groups to ensure equal employment opportunities and representation. In 2017, 27163 designated employers reported employment equity for 7,299,428 employees by province, business type, and sector. Gauteng employers reported 50.6% of the total number of employees. The Employment Equity Amendment (EE Amendment) Bill of 2019 allows sector-specific employment equity targets and Section 53, which requires employers to comply with the Act, to improve administration and compliance. In October 2018, NEDLAC Social Partners held public hearings on the amendments.

The CEE considered public comments and sector targets for the 2019–2020 financial year and the next Parliament after the May 2019 elections. The EAP assesses employers' underrepresentation of designated groups and sets numerical diversity goals and targets. During 2018, 27,485 designated employers reported covering 7,415,876 employees and 27 163 employment equity reports were submitted, up 320 (1.2%) and 116 447 employees (1.6%) from 2017. The amendments empowered the Minister to regulate employment equity sector targets for designated groups, ensure equitable representation of suitably qualified people, and reduce regulatory burden on small employers (less than 50 employees).

The Commission for Employment Equity and B-BBEE Act signed a memorandum of understanding to improve education, awareness, and enforcement to accelerate workplace and economic transformation. During this reporting period of 2019 – 2020 designated employer EE reports decreased by 1.3% from 2018 to 2019, despite a 1.8% decrease in reports. Compared to 2017, reports decreased but employees covered increased. In February 2020, the Cabinet approved the Employment Equity Amendment Bill and Draft Regulations.

The notable decrease of 1.8% from designated employer EE reports from 2019 to 2020 correlated with the 73.1% of deregistered employers no longer designated due to lower annual turnover or employee count.

The COVID – 19 pandemic and economy may have cut even designated employer workforces. The Employment Equity Amendment Bill, 2020, was published for public comment in February 2021, according to the 2021-2022 annual report. After public hearings and written submissions, the Committee on Employment and Labour referred the Bill to the National Assembly. The National Council of Provinces (NCOP) Select Committee released the EE Amendment Bill for public comment in December 2021 after receiving it in November 2021. In March 2022, the Department of Labour and Employment (DEL) answered all Select Committee questions.

Designated employers submitted 27,017 employment equity reports in 2021, covering 7,079,355 employees. Reports rose 1.4% and employees covered 0.3% from 2020 to 2021.

5.2. Impact of COVID – 19 pandemic on the implementation of EEA

On March 23, 2020, South Africa instituted a national lockdown to contain the COVID-19 pandemic. The Central Employment Exchange (CEE) examined how COVID-19 affected the European Economic Area (EEA) and its needs. On May 4, 2020, the CEE advised designated employers on compliance. COVID-19 devastated economic growth, job creation, and retention, according to the CEE. Organisations were compelled to investigate and compile COVID-19 Response and Recovery Plans for Business Continuity.

The CEE advised designated employers to follow guidelines to implement employment equity in the workplace since annual employment equity targets were inevitable. Employers were urged to follow employment laws during organisational restructuring and configuration to avoid unfair treatment and discrimination. If they cannot meet their 2020 EE targets, they should consult with EE Consultative Forums to revise their plans. COVID-19's impact on the labour market and society must be assessed by employers' annual EE Reports from September 2020 to January 2021. Before August 2020, employers were requested to write to the Director-General of the Department of Employment and Labour explaining why they cannot submit an EE Report.

Mergers/acquisitions, labour court orders, liquidations/judicial winding, insolvency, and others require EE14 forms. Proof should have must accompanied the EEA14 forms (Communication, 2020).

Since March 2020, the CEE has tracked Covid-19's impact on Employment Equity Act implementation using Director-General Notifications for failing to submit EE Reports (Kabinde et al., 2022).

5.3. The future of Employment Equity in South Africa

An article posted on the www.labournet.com website on the 20th of September 2022 sums up the question regarding the future of EE in South Africa.

The Employment Equity Amendments, formerly the "Proposed Employment Equity Amendments," were passed into law on May 17, 2022, and await the President's signature.

The amendments redefine "Designated Employer" and require an Employment Equity Compliance Certificate. Sectoral targets are set by the Minister with CEE input. The B-BBEE Act has targets and a compliance certificate, like the amendments.

The Employment Equity Act is enforceable, so it has more impact. The 1998 Act's main purpose is crucial to understanding the Department of Employment and Labour's (DoEL) view on transformation in South Africa. The Act considers past discriminatory laws and their effects on designated groups to provide equal opportunity and fair working environments for all races and genders.

The amendments are expected to end 22 years of direct employer control over business transformation. The 22nd Employment Equity Annual Report outlines DoEL goals.

The CEE's publication highlights employers' challenges in South Africa's 5-year EEA transformation. The goals are to advise the Minister on the EEA, mobilize stakeholders for employment equity compliance, empower workers to enforce their rights, empower employers to lead the transformation, and monitor, evaluate, and report on employment equity.

The DoEL and CEE's analysis of Employment Equity reports from 2019 to 2021 shows recurring themes that support the DoEL's EE Act reforms. White and Indian people are overrepresented in all occupations, while African people are underrepresented in all genders. Senior positions are still dominated by foreign nationals. Africans outnumber Whites and Indians in junior and entry-level jobs.

Given the number of disabled learnership providers and learners in South Africa, the representation of permanent disabled employees is concerning.

Employers still reporting barriers indicating unfair discrimination across policies, procedures, and practices worries the DoEL. The CEE thinks South Africa's transformation is slow because many organizations identify barriers that hurt designated groups or don't analyse and fix them. The report urges employers to identify and remove these barriers to ensure equal employment.

The Department of Labour and Employment (DoEL) and the National Minimum Wage Commission are reviewing remuneration sections for income differentials as part of new Employment Equity Act amendments to address these barriers.

Infrastructure, education, and competition have slowed EE. Infrastructure supports economic stability and growth, while education and accessibility pressure the private sector to train qualified workers. Competitors hiring skilled workers may blame the private sector, making South Africa's rainbow nation goal unaccountable.

The EEA amendments are intimidating for employers, and designated employers will be targeted more than ever. Employment Equity must be implemented and monitored strategically.

Employers must create a 5-year Employment Equity Plan to meet sectoral targets, with greater scrutiny on reasons for failure. South African employers must upskill their workforce using government funding and training plans and retain and develop existing employees through succession planning, promotions, and replacement. Employers must also meet employee retention and development needs.

Natural attrition requires succession planning to retain skilled workers. The DoEL and CEE emphasise representing disabled workers and amending the EEA. Refine the EEA1 document completion procedures should encourage employees to disclose disabilities. To raise disability awareness, employers should review diversity and inclusivity programs. According to the DoEL and CEE, the EEA will become stricter, and employers must focus on strategic workforce management and eliminating unfair discrimination (Labournet, 2022).

6. Conclusion

6.1. Summary of key points

The key points as takeaways in this paper are the following:

- The response of the EEA on gender disparities in South Africa
- The alignment of the B – BBEEA with the EEA in order to response to the transformational agenda within the South African economy;
- Monitoring of the changes brought about the amendments of the EEA of 1998 and the accompanying regulations;
- Ensuring that industry bodies, the South African Government, trade unions and businesses all have a focused approach towards the implementation of the EEA in South Africa in order to address the triple challenges of inequality, poverty and unemployment.

6.2. Importance of Employment Equity in South Africa's future

The Employment Equity Act's purpose is its importance. South Africa's diversity necessitates fair and equal representation to ensure that all citizens have access to employment. Fair employment should first reduce unemployment. Secondly, fair and equitable workforce access helps businesses hire the best candidates for open positions based on merit rather than demographics. Merit-based hiring improves workforce quality. This improves quality and builds trust in South African businesses locally and internationally.

Companies must comply with BBBEE codes of good practice for turnover and staffing. The BBBEE process relies on the submission to assess a company's employment equity performance. Designated companies must submit their employment equity annually by law. Non-compliance also lowers BBBEE management control element scores.

The Employment Equity Act could raise employment standards. This in return will improve South African business quality and trust over time. This could stabilize and improve our economy, which is important for those who depend on fairness for employment and development.

6.3. Call to action for continued progress towards Employment Equity

South Africa's Employment Equity Amendment Act 4 of 2022, passed by Parliament on 17 May 2022, promotes workplace diversity and equality.

President Cyril Ramaphosa signed the Employment Equity Amendment Act 4 of 2022 into law. The Employment Equity Act of 1998 (Act 55 of 1998) is amended to promote workplace diversity and equality. The President has not announced the effective date.

The amendments reduce the administrative burden on smaller employers by applying certain Employment Equity Act sections to fewer employers. The amendments set sectoral numerical targets to ensure race, gender, and disability representation at all occupational levels. On September 1, 2023, the amended Employment Equity (EE) Act will help transform South African workplaces. Section 53 of the amended EE Act of 1998 allows the Employment and Labour Minister to set sector-specific EE targets and compliance criteria for EE Compliance Certificates.

Except for the South African National Defence Force, National Intelligence Agency, and Secret Services, the Employment Equity Act (EEA) applies to all South African employers and employees. The EEA applies to all employers (except those above), but certain sections only apply to designated employers.

The EEA amendments will change the definition of "designated employer" to limit these sections to a smaller group of employers and reduce the administrative burden on smaller employers. The amendments empower the Minister of Labour and Employment to set numerical employment equity targets for each national economic sector.

The numerical targets ensure equitable workplace representation of suitably qualified people from historically disadvantaged groups based on race, gender, and disability at all occupational levels (Cliffe Dekker Hofmeyr, 2023) (MENA Report, 2022).

References

Archibong, U., Adejumo, O. & Phil, D. 2013. Affirmative Act ion in South Africa Are We Creating New Casualties? *Journal of Psychological issues in organizational culture*, 3(1): 14–27.

Bophelo Mtezuka. 2017. The Employment Equity Act and Racial Inequality in South Africa: Evidence from the Top Management Level in the Private Sector. *University of Johannesburg*, 87(1,2): 149–200.

CEE. 2002. Commission for Employment Equity Report 1999 - 2001. : 1–100. http://www.labour.gov.za/DOL/downloads/documents/annual-reports/employment-equity/1999-2001/CEE Annual Report.pdf.

Chief Directorate of Communication Department of Labour, for the C. for E.E. 2002. *Commission for Employment Equity Annual Report 2002 - 2003*.

Clarke, J. 2011. What is a systematic review. *Evidence-Based Nursing*, 14(3): 64.

Cliffe Dekker Hofmeyr. 2023. Q&A on the Employment Equity Amendment. *https://www.cliffedekkerhofmeyr.com/en/news/publications/2023/Practice/Employment/employment-law-alert-17-april-QA-on-the-employment-equity-amendment*.

Communication, D. of L.C.D. of. 2020. *21st Commission for Employment Equity (CEE) Annual Report*.

Creswell, J. 2012. *Educational research: Planning, conducting, and evaluating quantitative and qualitative research*. 4th ed. Pearson Education.

Department of Labour. 2014. Employment Equity Amendment Act, 2013. *Government Gazette*, 583(37238): 1–12. http://www.labour.gov.za/DocumentCenter/Acts/Employment Equity/Amendment/Ammended Employment Equity Act gazetted on the 16 January 2014.pdf.

Fashoyin, T. 1998. Industrial Relations in Southern Africa: The Challenge of Change. *Southern Africa Multidisciplinary Advisory Team International Labour Organization Harare, Zimbabwe*, (August).

Flowerday, W.T., Rankin, N. & Schöer, V. 2016. Continuity and Change in South African Labor Market Regulations : the Impact of Employment Equity Act of 1998 on Employment Strategies of Firms . *Swiss Programme for Research on Global Issues for Development.*

Government of South Africa. 1998. Commission for Employment Equity. *Government of South Africa.*

Kabinde, T., Chagonda, T., Mgolodela, Z.P., Tsebe, P. & Mvuma, M. 2022. 22nd Commission for Employment Equity (CEE): Annual Report (2021-2022). *Government Printers.*

Labour Department of Republic of South Africa. 2022. Summary of the Employment Equity Act 55 of 1998, as amended issued in terms of section 25 (1). *South African Government*, 25(1): 1–6.

Labournet. 2022. The Future of Employment Equity. *https://www.labournet.com/the-future-of-employment-equity/.*

Liu, X. 2016. A Literature Review on the Definition of Corruption and Factors Affecting the Risk of Corruption. *Open Journal of Social Sciences*, 04(06): 171–177.

MENA Report. 2022. South Africa : Employment and labour on 24 years of Employment Equity Act inequity in South African workplaces. *London.*

Nunn, J. & Chang, S. 2020. What are systematic reviews? *WikiJournal of Medicine*, 7(1): 1–11.

Nxesi, W.T. 2022. Employment Equity Act: Code of Good Practice on the Prevention and Elimination of Harassment in the Workplace. *Department of Employment and Labour*, (43630): 31. www.gpwonline.co.za.

Nzima, D. & Duma, V. 2014. The Employment Equity Act (EEA) as an instrument for Employment Equity in the South African labor market. *Mediterranean Journal of Social Sciences*, 5(9): 578–582.

Omar, F. & Kiley, J.D. 2022. Employment equity and employee morale at a selected public service organisation in Cape Town, South Africa. *SA Journal of Human Resource Management*, 20(55): 1–13.

Oosthuizen, R.M. & Naidoo, V. 2010. Attitudes towards and experience of employment equity. *SA Journal of Industrial Psychology*, 36(1): 0–9.

Republic of South Africa. 2014. Employment Equity Amendment Act No. 47 of 2013. *Government Gazette*, 583(37238): 2–22. http://www.labour.gov.za/DOL/downloads/legislation/acts/employment-equity/eea_amend2014.pdf.

van de Rheede, J. 2020. The Black Economic Empowerment Act 53 of 2003 and the ways in which the commission of fronting practices affects the achievement of its objective. *African Journal of Democracy & Governance*, 7(1): 101–118.

Utete, R. 2022. Examining the relationship between employment equity implementation and employee performance at the workplace: Evidence from a leading organisation in South Africa. *International Journal of Research in Business and Social Science (2147- 4478)*, 11(8): 141–152.

Vaal University of Technology. 2022. Employment Equity. *Vaal University of Technology*, 17(2): 1–7.

www.ingramcontent.com/pod-product-compliance
Lightning Source LLC
LaVergne TN
LVHW051131210926
848482LV00001B/54